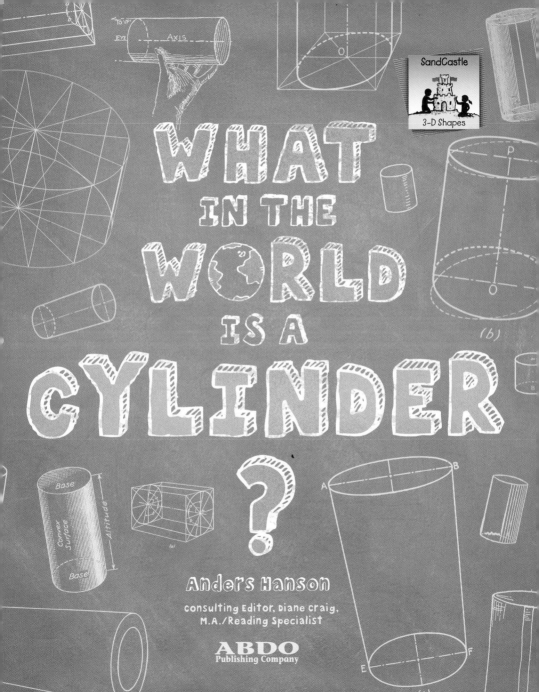

SandCastle
3-D Shapes

WHAT IN THE WORLD IS A CYLINDER?

Anders Hanson

Consulting Editor, Diane Craig,
M.A./Reading Specialist

ABDO
Publishing Company

Published by ABDO Publishing Company, 8000 West 78th Street, Edina, MN 55439.

Printed in the United States.
Editor: Pam Price
Curriculum Coordinator: Nancy Tuminelly
Cover and Interior Design and Production: Mighty Media
Photo Credits: JupiterImages Corporation, ShutterStock

Library of Congress Cataloging-in-Publication Data

Hanson, Anders, 1980-
  What in the world is a cylinder? / Anders Hanson.
    p. cm. -- (3-D shapes)
  ISBN 978-1-59928-888-8
  1. Cylinder (Mathematics)--Juvenile literature. 2. Shapes--Juvenile literature. 3. Geometry, Solid--
Juvenile literature. I. Title.

  QA491.H36 2007
  516'.154--dc22

                    2007006418

SandCastle™ Level: Transitional

Emerging Readers
(no flags)

Beginning Readers
(1 flag)

Transitional Readers
(2 flags)

Fluent Readers
(3 flags)

SandCastle™ would like to hear from you. Please send us your comments or questions.

sandcastle@abdopublishing.com

SandCastle™ books are created by a team of professional educators, reading specialists, and content developers around five essential components—phonemic awareness, phonics, vocabulary, text comprehension, and fluency—to assist young readers as they develop reading skills and strategies and increase their general knowledge. All books are written, reviewed, and leveled for guided reading, early reading intervention, and Accelerated Reader® programs for use in shared, guided, and independent reading and writing activities to support a balanced approach to literacy instruction. The SandCastle™ series has four levels that correspond to early literacy development. The levels are provided to help teachers and parents select appropriate books for young readers.

3-D shapes are all around us.

3-D stands for 3-dimensional.
It means that an object is not flat.

A cylinder is a 3-D shape.

BASE

BASE

A cylinder has two identical bases.

Most cylinders have bases that are circles or ovals.

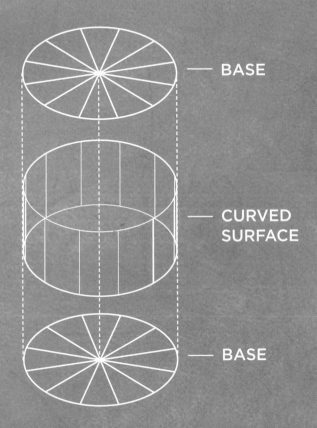

BASE

CURVED SURFACE

BASE

The bases are joined by a curved surface.

Cylinders are everywhere!

Gina drinks juice
with straws.

Straws are
cylinder shaped.

Emily uses a rolling pin
to flatten the dough.

The rolling pin is
shaped like a cylinder.

Suzy solves a
math problem.

The chalk is
cylinder shaped.

James is making
a finger painting.

The paint can
is shaped like
a cylinder.

Chelsea throws away litter in a park.

The garbage can is cylinder shaped.

Kara plays on a jungle gym.

The jungle gym bars are cylinders.

Liz plays in the slide at the park.

The slide is cylinder shaped.

Find the cylinder!

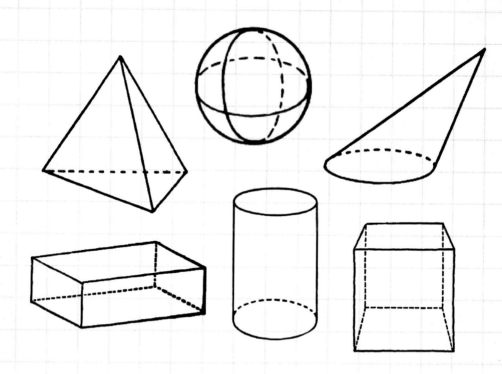

Which one of these 3-D shapes is a cylinder?

How many cylinders can you find in this photo?

Everyday cylinders

Take a look around you.
Do you see any cylinders?

How to draw a cylinder

1. Draw an oval.

2. Draw a half oval directly below it.

3. Connect the outer edges with straight lines.

Glossary

base – the side or face on which a 2-D or a 3-D figure can rest.

curve – to bend smoothly without any sharp angles.

dimensional – having a measurement of length, width, or thickness.

identical – exactly the same.

oval – a two-dimensional egg shape.

surface – the outside layer of something. In geometry, a surface is a shape with length and width but not thickness.

To see a complete list of SandCastle™ books and other nonfiction titles from ABDO Publishing Company, visit www.abdopublishing.com.
8000 West 78th Street, Edina, MN 55439 · 800-800-1312 · 952-831-1632 fax